# THE STO

# ELIZA
# HAMILTON

## A Biography Book for New Readers

Written by
**Natasha Wing**

Illustrated by
**Raquel Martín**

**ROCKRIDGE
PRESS**

To all the women who adopt and foster children. And to Aunt Jennifer and Aunt Andrea for believing in me.

Series Designer: Angela Navarra
Interior and Cover Designer: Sean Doyle
Art Producer: Tom Hood
Editor: Eliza Kirby
Production Editor: Nora Milman
Production Manager: Holly Haydash

Illustrations © Raquel Martin, 2021. Images on pp 50, 51 & 53 under license courtesy of Alamy.

Paperback ISBN: 978-1-64876-296-3 | eBook ISBN: 978-1-63807-279-9
R0

# ⇒ CONTENTS ⇐

# CHAPTER 1

# A FOUNDING MOTHER IS BORN

# Meet Elizabeth ☆ Schuyler Hamilton ☆

Elizabeth Schuyler [SKY-ler] loved being part of a big family. Her two sisters, Angelica and Peggy, were her best friends. The Schuyler children grew up in a loving home with both a mother and a father. Eliza later learned that not all kids were as lucky.

Eliza loved spending time with her parents, brothers, and sisters. However, some children did not have parents. Children whose parents have died are called **orphans**.

## MYTH & FACT

| MYTH | FACT |
| --- | --- |
| Eliza was born in a hospital. | There were no hospitals nearby until more than 40 years after she was born. |

Eliza later married an orphan named Alexander Hamilton. He was born on a Caribbean island and moved to the United States as a young man. Alexander had a hard childhood but grew up to be a great leader who helped form the **government** of the United States of America. Still, Eliza could not bear the thought that he had to take care of himself as a boy.

The Hamiltons had eight children. They also took in an orphan girl named Fanny. Eliza often wondered what would happen if a child did not

have a place to go. Who would take care of them? Who would give them a home?

Eliza spent much of her life answering those questions. As a **philanthropist**, she gave money, land, and much of her time to help children. She started a free school for kids. She also opened the first orphanage in New York City that was run by a private citizen. It is still there today!

Alexander is known as one of America's **Founding Fathers**. Eliza, with her big, kind heart, would also find her place in history as a beloved Founding Mother.

## ☆ **Eliza's America** ☆

Eliza was born on August 9, 1757, to Philip and Catherine "Kitty" Schuyler. The Schuylers were **wealthy** Dutch settlers. They owned land in upstate New York. New York was one of the original **13 colonies**.

People from other countries came to America. They called it the New World. They set up homes and started colonies. The king of England ruled the colonies. **Indigenous** Peoples already lived in America. They had their own governments.

**Colonists** lived off the land. They built their own homes. They raised cows and pigs. They grew garden crops and canned and stored their food for winter.

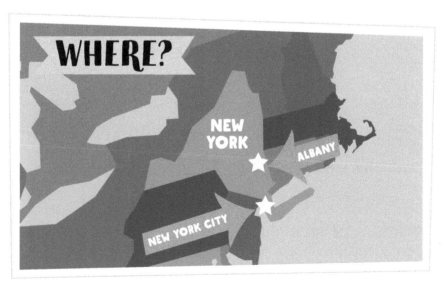

WHERE?

NEW YORK

ALBANY

NEW YORK CITY

They walked where they needed to go or traveled longer distances by horse and carriage.

In most families, the father ran the business while the mother ran the household. Men worked in farming, shipping, and selling goods. Mothers homeschooled their children and taught them the Bible. They sewed, cooked, and made soap. There was no electricity, so women made candles for light. Servants and **enslaved** Africans did chores, tended crops, and cared for children.

The Schuylers enslaved people who worked for them for no pay.

Girls stitched **samplers** to learn numbers and the alphabet. It was important for girls to have good sewing skills. They had to make and mend their own clothes. Eliza was very skilled at needlework.

Girls also learned how to string **wampum**. Wampum was used by Eastern Woodland Nations of Native Americans to record agreements, like the ones they made with colonists. Living on the frontier got Eliza ready for the challenges that lay ahead. And there were many!

# WHEN?

The Colony of New York is founded.

Elizabeth Schuyler is born.

**1664**

AUGUST 9,
**1757**

# CHAPTER 2
# THE EARLY YEARS

# Life Upstate

Eliza's mother, Catherine "Kitty" Van Rensselaer, came from **high society** in Albany, New York. In 1755, Kitty married Philip Schuyler, a military officer and businessman.

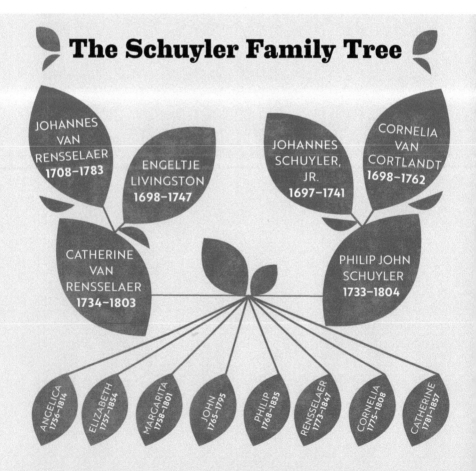

## The Schuyler Family Tree

JOHANNES VAN RENSSELAER
1708–1783

ENGELTJE LIVINGSTON
1698–1747

JOHANNES SCHUYLER, JR.
1697–1741

CORNELIA VAN CORTLANDT
1698–1762

CATHERINE VAN RENSSELAER
1734–1803

PHILIP JOHN SCHUYLER
1733–1804

ANGELICA
1756–1814

ELIZABETH
1757–1854

MARGARITA
1758–1801

JOHN
1765–1795

PHILIP
1768–1835

RENSSELAER
1773–1847

CORNELIA
1775–1808

CATHERINE
1781–1857

Kitty and Philip both came from wealthy Dutch families with political power.

Kitty gave birth to 15 children. Only eight survived. Eliza was the second-oldest child, between her sisters Angelica and Peggy. The three girls were as close as can be.

As the family grew, the Schuylers built a bigger house in Albany called the Pastures. Here Eliza learned to speak French and Dutch. She read the Bible and practiced her writing. The children played music and sang. Eliza played piano. The girls learned to cook and sew so they could someday run their own homes.

Eliza picked wild berries and rode her horse in the woods. She loved living near the Hudson River, where she canoed and skated when the river froze.

Important people, like future Founding Father Benjamin Franklin, often visited. The mansion became the hub of political talk—and talk of **revolution** was in the air!

## ☆ Whispers of Revolution ☆

When Eliza was almost 13, she and her father rode on horseback to a meeting with the Six Nations of the Haudenosaunee. The Native American leaders liked her father and grandfather because they helped keep the peace. They liked Eliza, too. She could make wampum and speak Iroquois. They gave her a name meaning "one of us." Good ties were important. There was always fear of attacks. But now there were even bigger fears about war with England.

The American colonists were unhappy. They did not want to pay taxes to England when they did not have a say in the government. They did not want to follow the king's laws.

On the night of April 18, 1775, 800 British soldiers, called Redcoats, marched out of Boston. They were heading to Concord to take weapons the colonists had hidden. Someone had to warn the colonists!

## MYTH  FACT

| MYTH | FACT |
|---|---|
| In the Midnight Ride from Boston, Paul Revere rode alone by horseback to warn Americans that the British were coming. | There were two more riders with Revere—William Dawes and Dr. Samuel Prescott. Revere was captured, so Dr. Prescott finished the ride. |

As the Redcoats passed Lexington—*bang*! Farmers shot at them from behind hedges and stone walls. In Concord, a battle broke out. The Redcoats lost and headed back to Boston. The American Revolution had begun!

Eliza was 18 at the time. As the colonies fought for independence, her father went to war to protect New York. The family prayed for his safe return. They hoped that the American soldiers could beat England and free the colonies.

The war brought fear, but it also brought young men to the Pastures. One story says a

young soldier named Alexander Hamilton came to the mansion in 1777 to deliver a message to Major General Schuyler. This may have been when Eliza and Alexander first met. Soon they would meet again.

## WHEN?

| The Schuyler family moves into the Pastures mansion. | Shots are fired at Lexington and Concord. | Declaration of Independence is written. | Eliza and Alexander may have first met at the mansion. |
| --- | --- | --- | --- |
| **1763** | APRIL 19, **1775** | **1776** | **1777** |

# CHAPTER 3
## INDEPENDENCE

# ✦ Eliza On Her Own ✦

In 1780, five years after the start of the American Revolution, the war was still going on.

Eliza went to Morristown, New Jersey, to visit her aunt Gertrude and uncle John. They lived near the camp where the Continental army stayed during winter and spring. It was exciting to meet the officers' wives, especially Martha Washington, the wife of General George Washington. Eliza was even more excited about her chances of meeting a husband. She was 22 years old and ready to start her own life.

One day, a handsome colonel came to Uncle John's house to deliver papers. It was Alexander Hamilton.

Eliza's sister Angelica arrived at camp in time for the winter ball. At the ball, Eliza and Alexander danced together. Eliza was in love! She wondered what Angelica thought of Alexander.

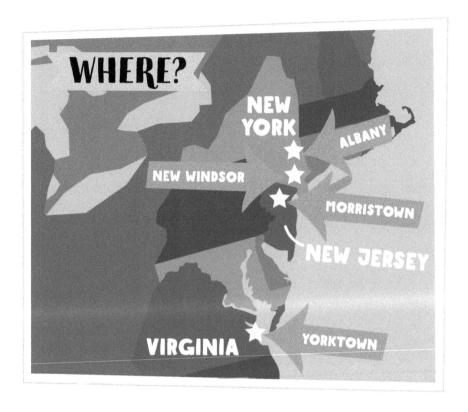

Angelica thought he was charming. But the sisters worried if their father and mother would approve. Alexander was a poor orphan and did not own any land.

Thankfully, both of Eliza's parents did approve. It was time to plan a wedding.

In June, Eliza went back to Albany and Alexander went to war. She and Alexander wrote love letters while they were apart. They wrote about missing each other, about their wedding plans, and about the war.

Finally, Alexander arrived in Albany. On December 14, Eliza and Alexander were married at the Schuyler mansion. The Schuylers welcomed Alexander into their family.

As America grew closer to breaking away from England, Eliza was becoming independent, too. She was ready to become the lady of the house.

## New Beginnings

The newlyweds stayed in the Schuyler mansion until the New Year, visiting with family and celebrating the holidays. Then it was back to work. Alexander met General Washington at his headquarters in New Windsor, New York. Eliza soon joined her husband.

Eliza had befriended Martha Washington at winter camp in New Jersey. Here at the general's headquarters, their friendship deepened.

Alexander talked with Eliza about his ideas for a new country. He wanted to unite the colonies, form a central government, and start a bank. Eliza helped him write down his ideas. She even gave him advice.

But Alexander was unhappy, and Eliza knew why. He wanted to be on the battlefield, not behind a desk. But Washington did not want his **assistant** to get hurt.

Alexander kept begging the general to let him go to battle. Finally, Washington said yes.

Eliza stayed with her family while Alexander was away. She wondered when she would ever be able to set up her own household. She also worried that her husband might be killed. Soon, she found out she was pregnant. Now she was even more worried for Alexander. He was about to become a father!

In October, Alexander joined General Washington in Yorktown, Virginia, to battle the British. The Continental army blocked the land. French warships blocked the sea.

JUMP
—IN THE—
THINK
TANK

If you were starting a new nation, what do you think it would need? Name three things.

19

Alexander's men charged! The British gave up.
The Americans had won.

Eliza was happy. Now her husband could
come home.

> 66 Mrs. Hamilton has given me a fine
> boy whose birth, as you may
> imagine, was attended with all the
> omens of future greatness.
>
> —ALEXANDER HAMILTON,
> in a letter to a friend 99

On January 22, 1782, their first son, Philip, was born. The birth of their baby and the birth of a nation marked two great beginnings for the Hamiltons.

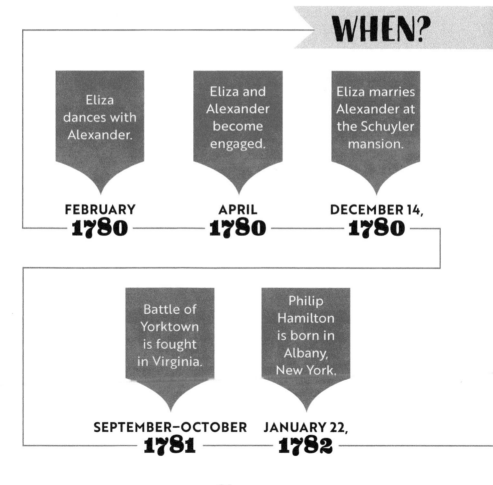

WHEN?

Eliza dances with Alexander.

Eliza and Alexander become engaged.

Eliza marries Alexander at the Schuyler mansion.

**FEBRUARY**
**1780**

**APRIL**
**1780**

**DECEMBER 14,**
**1780**

Battle of Yorktown is fought in Virginia.

Philip Hamilton is born in Albany, New York.

**SEPTEMBER–OCTOBER**
**1781**

**JANUARY 22,**
**1782**

# CHAPTER 4

# MRS. ELIZABETH HAMILTON

# A Statesman's Wife

Two years after Philip was born, the Hamiltons moved to New York City. Alexander set up the Bank of New York, New York's first bank. It still exists today.

Alexander next became a **lawyer**. He knew another lawyer named Aaron Burr. The two men had many things in common. They both opened their own law offices. Both men wanted to be in politics. They also knew many of the same friends. But instead of friendship, the two men developed a rivalry. It would last for years to come.

Still, these were times to celebrate! The war had ended. The 13 colonies united and formed a new government under the **Constitution**. George Washington was elected the first president. Alexander became his secretary of the treasury, a **statesman** in charge of money. Best of all, the Hamilton family was growing!

After Philip came Angelica, Alexander Jr., James, and John. Eliza also took in two-year-old Fanny Antill after the girl's mother died. As a mother, Eliza ran the household and took care of the children. As a statesman's wife, she also led a busy social life.

Meanwhile, Alexander was busy writing political papers and starting a banking system for the United States. Often Eliza helped him.

> 66 I sat up all night, copied out his writing, and the next morning, he carried it to President Washington and we had a bank. 99

## ☆ Hard Times ☆

Soon, however, Eliza's merry days in New York City took a turn for the worse. Alexander was away too much. Their marriage was in trouble.

Then in March 1801, Eliza's sister Peggy died.
Soon after, Eliza's oldest son, Philip, died in a **duel**.

Eliza and Alexander were very sad over the
loss of their son, but in time they were able to
find happiness again in their marriage. They had
three more children: William, Eliza, and Philip II.
Finally, they built their dream house in the country.

They called the house the Grange. It was built
on a hilltop with river views. It had barns, gardens,
and fruit trees. There was room for the kids to

run, just like Eliza had done at the Pastures. The Grange cost Alexander more money than he had, but it was worth it. He was happy tending to his gardens and spending time with his family.

Eliza had only spent a short time at her new home before more tragedy hit. First, her mother died. Then, something terrible happened.

The rivalry between Alexander and Aaron Burr took a turn for the worse. Burr was jealous of Alexander's success. Alexander disagreed with Burr's political ideas. He often spoke badly of Burr.

He made sure that when Burr ran for elections, he lost. He also called Burr a dangerous man. Burr wanted to defend his honor. He challenged Alexander to a duel.

On July 11, 1804, Alexander and Burr paced off. Many duels did not end in death and men were able to settle their differences. But this duel was different. Alexander fired his bullet, but it did not hit Burr. Burr's shot hit Alexander.

## JUMP
### —IN THE—
## THINK TANK

If you had a fight with your friend, how would you fix it?

Eliza and the children came to Alexander's bedside. She stayed with him until he died. She was too sad to go to his funeral. What would she do without him?

# WHEN?

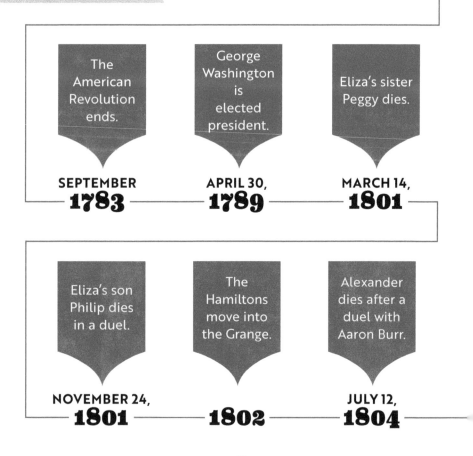

The American Revolution ends.

**SEPTEMBER 1783**

George Washington is elected president.

**APRIL 30, 1789**

Eliza's sister Peggy dies.

**MARCH 14, 1801**

Eliza's son Philip dies in a duel.

**NOVEMBER 24, 1801**

The Hamiltons move into the Grange.

**1802**

Alexander dies after a duel with Aaron Burr.

**JULY 12, 1804**

# CHAPTER 5

# A NEW PURPOSE

# Life After Alexander

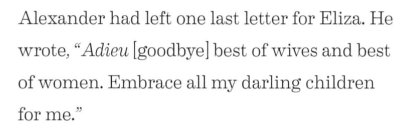

Alexander had left one last letter for Eliza. He wrote, "*Adieu* [goodbye] best of wives and best of women. Embrace all my darling children for me."

He had also left her with a lot of debt. The Hamiltons did not have much money saved. Eliza worried about the future of her older sons. They needed jobs, and the younger children needed schooling. She also wondered if she could afford to continue living in the Grange.

To save money, Eliza moved to a small rental home in New York City. Her father helped with some of the family's expenses. Eliza got her son Alexander Jr. a job in the city. John and James went to college there, too. Eliza was glad to have her children close by.

Eliza next set out to tell Alexander's story. She spoke with her father about finding an

author to write a book. Philip Schuyler had
kept his letters from Alexander. Eliza had piles
of Alexander's letters and political papers, too.
She would ask Alexander's friends to share
their memories.

Then, suddenly, Eliza's father died. Eliza
had to put the book on hold. Now that her
father could no longer help support her, there
was no other choice: She would have to sell
the Grange.

Alexander's friends raised money and bought the Grange. They sold it back to Eliza for half the price. Eliza was grateful. Now her younger children had a place to run and play. When her brother Philip's wife died, Eliza took in their two sons.

Being around children always gave Eliza joy. She started to wonder if she could do even more to help children.

## The Orphan Asylum Society

Eliza had suffered many tragedies over the last five years. Yet through her sadness she found her purpose.

Eliza met some women at church who were helping **widows** and motherless children. Isabella Graham was the president of the Society for the Relief of Poor Widows with Small Children. Isabella had taken in six orphans herself. She and her daughter, Joanna, along with another woman, Sarah Hoffman, were working on a new project. The women planned to create a home for orphaned children. Isabella and Sarah invited Eliza to join their mission.

On March 15, 1806, the women started the first orphanage in New York City that was run by a private citizen in a small house in Greenwich Village. It was called the Orphan Asylum Society of the City of New York. A safe home for orphans was a new idea. Before, orphans stayed in church housing or with a family member. They worked for their food and shelter and were often treated poorly.

WHERE?
NEW YORK
GREENWICH VILLAGE

Eliza poured her heart into helping these children. It was the perfect way to honor the orphans in her family: Alexander, Fanny, and her nephews.

She served as the second director, or vice president, and worked tirelessly for the orphanage.

> 66 [Eliza had] her own pitying, loving nature, blended with a rare sense of justice. All these she dedicated to the care of orphan children.
>
> —JESSIE BENTON FRÉMONT,
> Eliza's friend 99

She kept track of the orphanage's money. She asked for donations so the children could have shoes and Bibles. She even found jobs for older orphans. When the orphanage became too small, Eliza helped raise money to build a bigger one.

The orphanage still exists to this day. It is now called Graham Windham. It gives children a safe place to stay, health care, education, and, most importantly, family.

## JUMP —IN THE— THINK TANK

How can you help in your community? Could you pick up litter? Take shelter dogs for walks? Think of other ways you can lend a hand.

## WHEN?

| General Philip Schuyler dies. | Eliza's sister-in-law Sarah Rutsen Schuyler dies. | The orphanage opens. |
|---|---|---|
| **NOVEMBER 18, 1804** | **OCTOBER 24, 1805** | **MARCH 15, 1806** |

# CHAPTER 6

# ELIZA, BLAZING TRAILS

#  The Hamilton Free School

Eliza wanted to make sure every child had a chance at an education, just like her husband had. Alexander was lucky. People on the Caribbean island where he had grown up saw how smart he was. They had sent him to America and paid for him to go to college. Not all children were as lucky.

There was no free school in Washington Heights, a neighborhood near the Grange.

## JUMP
### —IN THE—
## THINK TANK

What causes do you believe in? Cleaning the ocean? Saving an endangered animal? What issues are important to you?

Parents had to pay to send their children to private schools. But many parents could not afford to. As a widow, Eliza had struggled to pay for her own children's education. She set out to open a free school in the neighborhood.

Eliza found a small house and turned it into a schoolhouse. Like the orphanage, the school soon became too small for all the children it needed to serve.

Eliza **donated** land in Washington Heights for a bigger school. Then she raised money to have the school built. In 1818, 12 years after the orphanage had opened, the new school opened. She named it the Hamilton Free School in honor of her husband.

The new school could hold more students. But
with the little money they had to run the school,
they could only pay one teacher. The teacher did
many jobs at the school.

Eliza was very busy running the orphanage.
Yet she still found time to visit the school and
hand out awards to students. The school stayed
open for almost 40 years.

# ⭐ Preserving Memories ⭐

In 1821, Eliza took over as first director of the orphanage. On top of running the orphanage and overseeing the school, Eliza took on another big project she had put aside for years: the publication of Alexander Hamilton's biography.

Long after his death, people were still spreading rumors about Alexander. Eliza wanted to protect his name. She wanted to

make sure people remembered him as a good man and an important statesman. She traveled to Long Island, New Jersey, and Virginia collecting his papers and letters. She asked people to share their stories about his character and good heart.

Eliza tried for a long time to find the right person to write Alexander's biography. Finally, Alexander's old friend Colonel Timothy Pickering agreed to write the book. With the help of her son John, the biography was finally published. People now knew how many important papers Alexander had written, including President George Washington's Farewell Address.

In the meantime, the Grange had become too costly to keep up. In 1833, Eliza sold it. She moved in with her son and daughter and their spouses.

## MYTH  FACT

| MYTH | FACT |
|---|---|
| Presidents always write their own speeches. | Most presidents have speechwriters to help them. Alexander wrote many speeches for George Washington. |

Eliza continued to stay involved with the orphanage until she was 91 years old. But this would not be her last project.

## WHEN?

| Hamilton Free School opens. | Eliza is promoted to first director of the orphanage. | Eliza sells the Grange. |
|---|---|---|
| **MARCH** | | **NOVEMBER** |
| **1818** | **1821** | **1833** |

CHAPTER 7

A LIFE WELL LIVED

# The White House Guest

Eliza had been first director at the orphanage for 27 years. She retired in 1848 when she was 91 years old. She then moved to Washington, DC, to live with her daughter. Here she lived out the rest of her life.

Eliza stayed as busy as ever. She often dined as an honored guest at the White House. She entertained everyone with her sharp mind and cheerfulness. President James K. Polk, the 11th president of the United States, even wrote in his diary about how charming she was.

There were a lot of visitors at Eliza's house as well. People wanted to meet someone who had lived through the American Revolution. Her nieces visited during winter social season, a time for parties and dances. Politicians came to pay their respects. One New Year's Day, Eliza had 200 visitors!

As one last project, Eliza helped Dolley Madison raise money to build the Washington Monument. Eliza and Dolley had met as young ladies, before the United States won its independence. Their husbands had both fought alongside General Washington. Now they were teaming up to pay tribute to the first president of the United States.

Unfortunately, Eliza did not live to see the monument completed.

## JUMP —IN THE— THINK TANK

Eliza knew many presidents throughout her lifetime. Which president would you like to meet? Why?

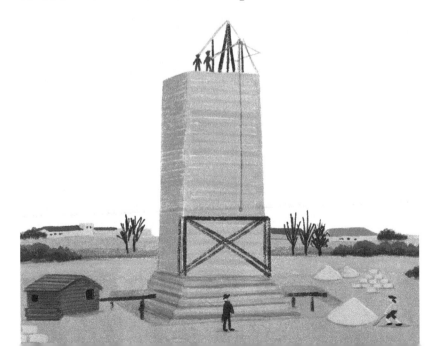

## MYTH  & FACT

| MYTH | FACT |
|------|------|
| The monument design was an **obelisk** shape from the beginning. | The monument was originally supposed to be a **pantheon**, or temple. |

On November 9, 1854, Eliza Hamilton died. She was 97 years old. Eliza outlived Alexander by 50 years. In those years, she gave so much to the country she loved.

## ☆ Not One Legacy, but Two

Eliza helped change the world during her long life. Most of the contributions she made were after Alexander had died.

As Alexander's wife, she helped him write the words that formed a new country. America went from 13 colonies ruled by the king of England to the United States—run by **democracy**.

Eliza was forever loyal to Alexander. By publishing his biography, she made sure everyone would remember how he shaped the new country's government. Historians, teachers, authors, and actors can be thankful for the information Eliza left behind for all to read. Eliza was even a lead character in the hit Broadway musical *Hamilton*!

By opening a safe home for orphans and a free school, she gave each child a chance at a better life. At Graham Windham in New York City, children still benefit from her work.

WHERE?

NEW YORK

NEW YORK CITY

PENNSYLVANIA

NEW JERSEY

MARYLAND

WASHINGTON, DC

Eliza was a pioneer, a tireless helper, and a keeper of history.

She truly was the "best of wives and the best of women."

## WHEN?

| Eliza moves to Washington, DC. | Cornerstone of the Washington Monument is laid. | Eliza dies at 97 years old. | The Washington Monument is completed. |
| --- | --- | --- | --- |
| **1848** | JULY 4, **1848** | NOVEMBER 9, **1854** | **1884** |

# CHAPTER 8

# SO...WHO WAS
# ELIZA
# HAMILTON
# ?

# ☆ Challenge Accepted! ☆

Now that you have learned about Eliza
Hamilton's long life as a Founding Mother and
philanthropist, let's test your new knowledge in
a little who, what, when, where, why, and how
quiz. Feel free to look back in the text to find the
answers if you need to, but try to remember first!

**When was Elizabeth
Schuyler born?**

A 1776
B 1780
C 1757
D 1700

**2** **What was the name of Eliza's
family home in Albany?**

A The Farm
B The Pastures
C Schuyler Hall
D Dutch Estates

**Who were the three Schuyler Sisters?**

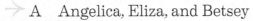

> A  Angelica, Eliza, and Betsey

> B  Catherine, Eliza, and Peggy

> C  Kitty, Angelica, and Eliza

> D  Angelica, Eliza, and Peggy

**4**  **Where did Eliza meet Alexander Hamilton?**

> A  At winter camp in New Jersey

> B  At school in New York City

> C  At the Grange

> D  At a dinner at the White House

**What was the name of the first orphan girl Eliza and Alexander took in?**

> A  Betsey

> B  Fanny

> C  Mary

> D  Peggy

### 6 How did Alexander Hamilton die?

→ A  Old age

→ B  Yellow fever

→ C  Gunshot in a duel

→ D  Killed in battle

### 7 Where is the orphanage Eliza started? In the city of:

→ A  New York City

→ B  Albany

→ C  Philadelphia

→ D  Washington, DC

### 8 Why did Eliza name her youngest son Philip?

→ A  To honor her father

→ B  It was Alexander's middle name

→ C  To honor her first son, Philip, killed in a duel

→ D  It was the name of her favorite horse

**9** Who helped Eliza publish the biography? Her son:

→ A John

→ B Alexander

→ C William

→ D James

**10** With whom did Eliza help raise money for the Washington Monument?

→ A Martha Washington

→ B Ulysses Grant

→ C Isabella Graham

→ D Dolley Madison

# ☆ Our World ☆

How has Eliza's work changed our world today? Let's look at a few things that have happened because of Elizabeth Hamilton.

→ Eliza saved Alexander Hamilton's letters and political papers. His biography helped people understand one of America's Founding Fathers as a person, and how important he was to the creation of the nation.

→ Eliza believed that all children should have families. She started an orphanage in New York City that still serves families in need today.

→ Because of Eliza's friendship with George Washington, she helped raise money to build one of the most iconic memorials in Washington, DC—the Washington Monument.

**JUMP —IN THE— THINK TANK FOR**

**⁻ MORE! ⁻**

Now let's think a bit more about what Eliza Hamilton did, the ways she changed how people treated poor children, and how she and her husband affected the world we live in today.

→ Eliza created a place where kids could feel safe. Where do you feel safe?

→ Eliza made sure Alexander was remembered by publishing a biography. Who would you write a biography about? What would you want people to remember most about this person?

# Glossary

**13 colonies:** The first colonies formed in what would become the United States

**assistant:** A person who gives aid to another; a helper

**colonists:** People who go to a foreign country and claim the land as their own

**Constitution:** A document written in 1787 that states the basic rules for how the United States must be run

**democracy:** A government ruled by the people

**donate:** To give as a way to help other people in need

**duel:** A contest between two people used to settle a disagreement, often with deadly weapons like guns or swords

**enslave:** To force a person to work without giving them freedom to choose and without paying them for their service

**Founding Fathers:** The men who helped create the rules and ideas that formed the United States of America

**government:** The system that controls and manages people who live in a particular place

**high society:** The fashionable rich

**Indigenous**: Original to a place; native

**lawyer**: A person whose job is to know all about the rules and laws of government

**obelisk**: A tall, thin, four-sided stone that rises to a pointed top

**orphan**: A young person who has no living parents

**orphanage**: Where orphans live

**pantheon**: A rectangular temple

**philanthropist**: A person who gives money and time to help others, especially by donating money to good causes

**revolution**: A fight against the ruling government

**sampler**: A piece of needlework used to practice stitches, letters, and numbers

**statesman**: A political leader who promotes the public good

**wampum**: A string of beads made of shells woven in belts and clothing, used by Eastern Woodland Indigenous Nations in ceremonies, to record agreements, or like money in trade

**wealthy**: Having plenty or being rich

**widow**: A woman whose spouse has died and who has not remarried

# Bibliography

Belviso, Meg and Pam Pollack. 2017. *Who Was Alexander Hamilton?* New York: Penguin Workshop.

Chernow, Ron. 2004. *Alexander Hamilton*. New York: Penguin Books.

Funiciello, Danielle. "Guest Blog: The Women of Schuyler Mansion." Hudson River Maritime Museum: History Blog, April 14, 2017. HRMM.org/history-blog/guest-blog-the-women-of-schuyler-mansion.

Graham-Windham.org. "Eliza's Story." Accessed June 7, 2021. Graham-Windham.org/elizas-story.

Kiger, Patrick J. "How Alexander Hamilton's Widow, Eliza, Carried on His Legacy." June 30, 2020. History.com/news/eliza-alexander-hamilton-legacy.

Mazzeo, Tilar J. 2018. *Eliza Hamilton: The Extraordinary Life and Times of the Wife of Alexander Hamilton*. New York: Gallery Books.

National Geographic Society. "Women and Children in Colonial America." Last updated April 28, 2020. NationalGeographic.org/encyclopedia/women -and-children-colonial-america.

National Park Service. "A Founding Father's Harlem Home." Last updated June 5, 2020. NPS.gov/hagr/index.htm.

New Netherland Institute. "Elizabeth Schuyler Hamilton [1757–1854]." Accessed June 7, 2021. NewNetherlandInstitute.org/history-and-heritage /dutch_americans/elizabeth-schuyler-hamilton.

Platt, Christine. 2020. *The Story of Alexander Hamilton*. Emeryville, California: Rockridge Press.

Syrett, Harold C., ed. 1961–1987. *The Papers of Alexander Hamilton*. 27 vols. New York: Columbia University Press.

# Acknowledgments

I would like to acknowledge the valuable work of Graham Windham. Founded on the mission of the women who opened New York City's first private orphanage, Graham Windham serves New York City youth and families.

# About the Author

**Natasha Wing** has been publishing children's books for 30 years. She has written biographies of Jackie Kennedy Onassis and artist Josef Albers and is particularly interested in the contributions of women to history. Natasha graduated from Arizona State University and continues to learn by writing nonfiction books.

# About the Illustrator

**Raquel Martín** is a Spanish illustrator from Barcelona based in the beautiful island of Minorca. Her work has appeared in different magazines and she has illustrated several picture books.

# WHO WILL INSPIRE YOU NEXT?

EXPLORE A WORLD OF HEROES AND ROLE MODELS IN
*THE STORY OF...* BIOGRAPHY SERIES FOR NEW READERS.

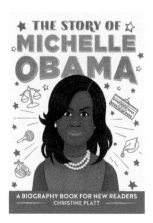

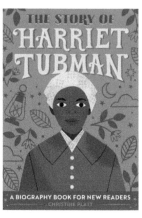

## LOOK FOR THIS SERIES
### WHEREVER BOOKS AND EBOOKS ARE SOLD

CPSIA information can be obtained
at www.ICGtesting.com
Printed in the USA
JSHW031905111121
20379JS00006B/66